D1276897

Helen's Eyes

Helen's Eyes

A Photobiography of

Annie Sullivan
Helen Keller's Teacher

❧

Marfé Ferguson Delano

NATIONAL GEOGRAPHIC

WASHINGTON, D.C.

For my smart, stubborn, spirited, and wonderfully silly sisters,
Karen Jo and Sherri, with love — MFD

2015 paperback edition ISBN: 978-1-4263-2222-8
2015 reinforced library binding ISBN: 978-1-4263-2236-5

STAFF FOR THIS BOOK

Nancy Laties Feresten, Vice President, Editor-in-Chief, Children's Books
Bea Jackson, Design and Illustrations Director, Children's Books
Jean Cantu, Illustrations Coordinator
Amy Shields, Executive Editor, Series, Children's Books
Jennifer Emmett, Project Editor
Marty Ittner, Designer
Callie Broaddus, Associate Designer
Lori Epstein, Senior Photo Editor
Charlotte Fullerton, Illustrations Editor
Paige Towler, Editorial Assistant
Carl Mehler, Director of Maps
Matthew Chwastyk, Map Research and Production
Jennifer A. Thornton, Managing Editor
R. Gary Colbert, Production Director
Lewis R. Bassford, Production Manager
Maryclare Tracy and Nicole Elliott, Manufacturing Managers
Susan Borke, Senior Vice President and Deputy General Counsel
Marla Conn, Education Consultant

PUBLISHED BY THE NATIONAL GEOGRAPHIC SOCIETY

Gary E. Knell, President and CEO
John M. Fahey, Chairman of the Board
Melina Gerosa Bellows, Chief Education Officer
Declan Moore, Chief Media Officer
Hector Sierra, Senior Vice President and General Manager, Book Division

SENIOR MANAGEMENT TEAM, KIDS PUBLISHING AND MEDIA

Nancy Laties Feresten, Senior Vice President; **Jennifer Emmett,** Vice
President, Editorial Director, Kids Books; **Julie Vosburgh Agnone,**
Vice President, Editorial Operations; **Rachel Buchholz,** Editor and Vice
President, *NG Kids* magazine; **Michelle Sullivan,** Vice President, Kids
Digital; **Eva Absher-Schantz,** Design Director; **Jay Sumner,** Photo Director;
Hannah August, Marketing Director; **R. Gary Colbert,** Production Director

DIGITAL

Anne McCormack, Director; **Laura Goertzel, Sara Zeglin,** Producers; **Emma
Rigney,** Creative Producer; **Brian Ford,** Video Producer; **Bianca Bowman,**
Assistant Producer; **Natalie Jones,** Senior Product Manager

National Geographic supports K–12 educators with ELA Common Core
Resources. Visit natgeoed.org/commoncore for more information.

Printed in China
15/RRDS/1

ACKNOWLEDGMENTS

The author thanks Jan Seymour-Ford for her gracious and expert
assistance during my research trip to Perkins. Theta luv to Tammy
Wilson Roberts for putting me up for the night. Thank you to
Elizabeth Hargrove for a delightful tour of Ivy Green. A big hug to my
cousin Charlene Flournoy and her husband, Tim, for their wonderful
southern hospitality. Enormous thanks to my patient editor, Jennifer
Emmett, and the rest of the National Geographic Children's Book
department. I am also grateful to Marty Ittner and Charlotte
Fullerton. And to my new friend Deborah Heiligman—thanks for all
the support and advice and encouragement and laughter.

The publisher thanks Jan Seymour-Ford, Research Librarian, Perkins
School for the Blind, for her expert review of the book.

The body text of the book is set in Mrs. Eaves.
The display text is set in Dalliance and Officina Sans

FRONT COVER: Annie Sullivan stands behind Helen Keller in this
portrait made around 1893. A chart of braille symbols appears in the
background.

SPINE: Helen Keller's hands demonstrating the manual alphabet

BACK COVER: Annie and Helen and their dog perch in a favorite
reading spot near their home in Wrentham, Massachusetts, in 1904.
Helen is reading Annie's lips with her hand as Annie reads a book aloud.

HALF-TITLE PAGE: Braille text that reads (three times):
Helen's Eyes
A Photobiography of Annie Sullivan,
Helen Keller's Teacher
by Marfé Ferguson Delano

TITLE PAGE: Annie Sullivan (right) and Helen Keller play chess
around 1900. They use a special chessboard that enables blind
players to feel the layout of the board.

OPPOSITE PAGE: Annie Sullivan (right) and Helen Keller in a portrait
made around 1895. In 1980, the U.S. Postal Service issued a stamp
based on this picture. The stamp is shown on page 62 of this book.

The National Geographic Society is one of the world's largest
nonprofit scientific and educational organizations. Founded
in 1888 to "increase and diffuse geographic knowledge,"
the Society's mission is to inspire people to care about the
planet. It reaches more than 400 million people worldwide
each month through its official journal, *National Geographic,*
and other magazines; National Geographic Channel;
television documentaries; music; radio; films; books; DVDs; maps; exhibitions;
live events; school publishing programs; interactive media; and merchandise.
National Geographic has funded more than 10,000 scientific research, conser-
vation, and exploration projects and supports an education program promoting
geographic literacy.

For more information, please visit nationalgeographic.com,
call 1-800-NGS LINE (647-5463), or write to the following address:

NATIONAL GEOGRAPHIC SOCIETY
1145 17th Street N.W.
Washington, D.C. 20036-4688 U.S.A.

Visit us online at nationalgeographic.com/books

For librarians and teachers: ngchildrensbooks.org

More for kids from National Geographic: kids.nationalgeographic.com

For information about special discounts for bulk purchases, please
contact National Geographic Books Special Sales: ngspecsales@ngs.org

For rights or permissions inquiries, please contact National Geographic
Books Subsidiary Rights: ngbookrights@ngs.org

"I know that the education of this child will be the distinguishing event of my life, if I have the brains and perseverance to accomplish it."

In a photograph taken when she was about 34, Annie Sullivan reads a book to Helen Keller by finger-spelling the words into Helen's hand. Helen later wrote that Teacher, as she called Annie, "was eyes and ears for me in the acquisition of language."

Foreword

I remember the day quite well. It was a cool, crisp, fall day in 1979. I was in the fourth grade at Northside Middle School in Tuscumbia, Alabama. My first real assignment for the school year was to present a program to my classmates on the person I admired the most—Helen Keller, my great grand aunt. Although Helen died in 1968, and none of my classmates actually knew her personally, we all knew her story quite well. So, I decided to make the day even more exciting by inviting my grandmother, Helen Keller's niece, Patty Tyson Johnson, to our class to tell us of her memories of Helen Keller.

In vivid detail my grandmother told my class story after story of her visits with the world famous Helen Keller. She commented on how Helen Keller was received with a massive outpouring of love and admiration wherever she went. She also explained to the class how Helen's personal victory over darkness and despair had turned her life and her ambitions to the service of others.

As my teacher asked the class if anyone had any questions, a girl in the back of my class asked my grandmother how Helen Keller was able to do all these things being both deaf and blind. My grandmother responded by saying two words: Annie Sullivan. She went on to explain that it was important to remember that without the help of her teacher, Annie Sullivan, Helen Keller would have never succeeded as she did. She relied a great deal on her teacher, who had not only broken through Helen's dark and silent world when Helen was just seven years old, but who also accompanied Helen Keller almost everywhere she went for the next 50 years.

Since that time, I have realized that many people are familiar with Annie Sullivan's outstanding achievements teaching Helen Keller, but few people know the story behind the "miracle worker." Perhaps the greatest miracle in Annie Sullivan's life was her conquest over her own handicaps—a very cruel and poor childhood, and partial blindness caused by trachoma. Although my grandmother has been gone from this world for nearly 12 years, her last words from that day still echo in my ears: "History can be changed when one person says, 'What can someone like me do?'"

Keller Johnson Thompson

Imagine a world without sight or sound. A world without communication, knowledge, or hope. A world where frustration makes you wild and there's no such thing as self-control. This was Helen Keller's world until Annie Sullivan entered it. By unlocking the world of language for Helen, Annie uncovered a gifted girl who inspired a nation with her courage and determination to live life to the fullest despite being both blind and deaf. Annie became known as the "miracle worker." She showed the world what teaching, at its best, can do. Considering the obstacles she had to overcome in her own childhood, however, one of the most miraculous things about Annie Sullivan is that she ever became a teacher at all.

Annie was born on April 14, 1866, in a small village in western Massachusetts called Feeding Hills. Her parents, Alice and Thomas Sullivan, were among the hundreds of thousands of poor Irish immigrants who flocked to America in the 19th century in search of a better life. But the Sullivan family's life in Feeding Hills was one of crushing poverty. Thomas Sullivan was an unskilled laborer who could not read or write. An alcoholic with an explosive temper, he drank away much of the little money that he earned working as a farmhand. He had his charming moments, when he sang Irish songs and told Annie tales of the legendary Little People and fairy folk back in Ireland. Other times he beat Annie so severely that her mother, Alice, tried to hide the girl from him.

When Annie was about five years old, her eyes began to bother her. They became red and swollen and clouded over, and they felt scratchy

This is the first known photograph of Annie Sullivan, taken when she was about 15. The view in the background shows the area in western Massachusetts where Annie spent her first ten years.

"I doubt if life or for that matter eternity
is long enough to erase the errors and
ugly blots scored upon my mind by those
dismal years from 8 to 14."

and sore. One of Annie's earliest memories was of someone saying about her, "She would be so pretty if it were not for her eyes." The problem with Annie's eyes was later diagnosed as a contagious eye disease called trachoma. It began gradually to destroy her vision. Annie would battle against blindness the rest of her life.

Alice Sullivan died from tuberculosis when Annie was about eight years old. Thomas Sullivan was left with three children: Annie, the oldest, who had a quick temper of her own by this time; five-year-old Jimmie, who had a crippling lump on his hip caused by tuberculosis; and Mary, a strong and healthy toddler.

Thomas Sullivan eventually abandoned his children, leaving his relatives to support them. Healthy, lovable little Mary was taken in by an aunt. But no one wanted hot-headed, half-blind Annie and sickly, lame Jimmie. So the two of them were sent to live in the state-run poorhouse, or almshouse, in Tewksbury, Massachusetts. It was a place for poor and needy people who had nowhere else to go.

At the Tewksbury train station, Annie and Jimmie were met by a dark, windowless carriage called a Black Maria, a vehicle usually used by police to take criminals to jail. It delivered the tired and bewildered children to the Tewksbury Almshouse on February 22, 1876. Annie was not quite ten years old.

The institution had no special place for orphaned children. Women and girls lived in one section, men and boys in another. But Annie kicked up such a fuss when the authorities tried to separate her

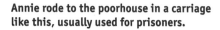

Annie rode to the poorhouse in a carriage like this, usually used for prisoners.

The ward that Annie and Jimmie Sullivan lived in at the Tewksbury Almshouse was probably similar to the men's ward shown above. The ledger entry below records the children's admission to the institution in 1876.

from Jimmie that they were allowed to stay together. They were sent to a ward that housed mostly elderly women. The children spent their first night there in the "dead house," a room at the end of the ward where dead bodies were prepared for burial.

Death was all too common at Tewksbury, which was run down, filthy, and overcrowded. Many of the inmates were diseased or mentally ill or both. Some were drunks or criminals. Some were violent. Few were fit company for children.

Still, Annie and Jimmie made the best of things. At least they were together. They slept side by side on cots, and they made the rat-infested dead house their playroom. Many years later, Annie recalled that

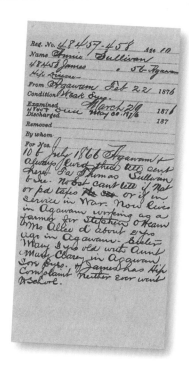

"Jimmie used to tease the rats with long spills [rolls] of paper made from the pages of the Police Gazette and used to shriek with delight when one of them leapt into the room and frightened the patients."

Jimmie's health went from bad to worse at Tewksbury. He died three months after they arrived. "I must have been sound asleep when Jimmie died, for I didn't hear them roll his bed into the dead house," Annie remembered. "Suddenly I missed Jimmie's bed. The black, empty space where it had been filled me with wild fear." After her brother's funeral, Annie recalled, "I longed desperately to die. I believe very few children have ever been so completely left alone as I was."

Annie lived behind the Tewksbury gates for four more years. She learned to fend for herself and to steer clear of the troublemakers. She watched with fascination as other inmates—many of them poor Irish, like herself—laughed and loved and drank and argued and fought and stole and sickened and died. "Very much of what I remember about Tewksbury is indecent, cruel…[and] gruesome in the light of grown-up experience," she remarked many years later. But as a child, she said, "Everything interested me. I was not shocked…or troubled by what happened.… People behaved like that—that was all that there was to it. It was all the life I knew. Things impressed themselves on me because I had a receptive mind. Curiosity kept me alert and keen to know everything."

Annie was twice sent to hospitals for eye operations, but her vision continued to decline. She could see nothing but "bright colors dancing in a perpetual and bewildering procession." When one of the other almshouse inmates told Annie that there were such things as schools for blind children, Annie made up her mind that one day she would go to such a school.

She was 14 years old when she finally got the chance. Annie learned that a group of inspectors, led by a Mr. Frank Sanborn, were coming to investigate the notorious conditions at Tewksbury. When they

Annie Sullivan lived most of her life in Massachusetts, at the places shown here. When she moved to Alabama in 1887, she found it hard to adapt to the southern climate. "My head aches a good deal, and I cannot sleep," she wrote a friend back in Boston. "I think perhaps it is the heat....You don't know how hot it is."

arrived, she screwed up her courage, threw herself into their midst, and cried, "Mr. Sanborn, Mr. Sanborn, I want to go to school!"

Annie got her wish. She was soon transferred to the Perkins Institution for the Blind in Boston. She found it far from a dream come true, however. Used to rough and rude Tewksbury, she had a hard time adjusting to quiet, polite Perkins. "For a long time," Annie noted, "I was like a round peg in a square hole at Perkins. I was large for my age, and utterly unacquainted with the usages of civilized people. In some ways I was as mature as a woman, in others as undeveloped as a child."

Most of the students at the school came from middle-class or well-to-do families. Annie didn't even own a nightgown or a hairbrush when she arrived. She couldn't read or write, and she didn't know her own birthday. Her Irish accent, ignorance, and coarse manners caused many of the other girls—and even some of the teachers—to ridicule her. Fourteen years old, they taunted, and she couldn't even spell her name or thread

Laura Bridgman, shown here at about age 16, was the first deaf-blind person to be successfully educated in the United States. Dr. Samuel Gridley Howe (top) taught her the manual alphabet, which was invented by Spanish monks so that they could communicate without breaking their vow of silence. The poster in the background features Helen Keller's hands demonstrating the manual alphabet.

a needle! Annie burned with anger and shame. She even found herself homesick for Tewksbury.

Annie was tough, however, and she hungered for an education. The humiliation only made her more determined to excel as a student. She refused to let the others know that their remarks hurt her. Instead she flared back. "When is your brain awake?" demanded her math teacher one day. "When I leave your class," Annie retorted. Annie's fiery temper and tart tongue nearly got her expelled more than once. But Perkins director Michael Anagnos, who nicknamed Annie "Miss Spitfire," didn't have the heart to send her back to the poorhouse, so she was allowed to stay. "Because I was ignorant, and felt inferior, I pretended that I was scornful and contemptuous of everybody," Annie remembered. "As a matter of fact I was extremely unhappy. My mind was a question mark, my heart a frustration."

Annie's incredible intelligence soon became clear. She quickly learned the alphabet using raised-letter type, which was felt with the fingertips. She also learned braille, a system of writing and printing for blind people that uses patterns of raised dots to represent letters and numbers. In a surprisingly short time, she bridged the academic gap between herself and other students her age. Eventually, she began to make friends at Perkins. She became especially close with Mrs. Sophia Hopkins, the house mother of the cottage where she lived. She also got to know a Perkins resident named Laura Bridgman.

Born in 1829, Laura Bridgman had been blind and deaf since suffering scarlet fever at age two. When she was seven, she was brought to Perkins by its first director, Dr. Samuel Gridley Howe. The challenge of educating her intrigued him. Up to this time, efforts to educate deaf-blind people had failed.

Howe began introducing Laura to language by giving her an object, such as a spoon, with its name pasted on it in raised letters. After a few weeks Laura learned to associate the raised-letter words with the objects—she realized that things have names. After this breakthrough, Howe taught her the manual alphabet, in which the letters are represented by finger positions. The "talker" spells words into the palm of the "listener," who feels the finger movements. Laura soon learned to communicate with others through finger-spelling.

Called a braillewriter, this machine was used for typing out documents in braille. Its six keys correspond to the six dots used in braille symbols. Users pushed down one or more of the keys to make the raised patterns on paper.

News of Laura Bridgman's accomplishments spread around the world. She and Howe became celebrities. Laura never learned to function in the world outside Perkins, however. She lived at the school for the rest of her life, teaching sewing and needlework. She was 50 years old when Annie met her.

Kindergarten students enjoy playing with geometric shapes at the Perkins Institution for the Blind in 1900. When Annie Sullivan first entered the school as a 14-year-old in 1880, other students — and some teachers — made fun of her because she was uneducated. "When I made mistakes," Annie later recalled, "the teachers ridiculed me in a way they would never have dreamed of doing if I were a young child."

"For a long time I was like a round peg in a square hole at Perkins. I was large for my age, and utterly unacquainted with the usages of civilized people. In some ways I was as mature as a woman, in others as undeveloped as a child."

Annie learned the manual alphabet so that she could chat with Laura. It would become a very important skill for her just a few years later.

During her time at Perkins, Annie had two operations on her eyes. They changed her life, restoring her vision to the point that she could read printed materials. Although her eyes tired easily, she began to devour book after book, and she developed a life-long passion for reading and literature. Annie also gave herself an aristocratic-sounding middle name, "Mansfield," which a friend told her was used by wealthy Irish people.

On June 1, 1886, at the age of 20, "Anne Mansfield Sullivan" graduated from Perkins as the valedictorian, or top-ranked student, of her class. Her determination and hard work had paid off. Dressed in a beautiful white dress made for her by Mrs. Hopkins, she delivered her valedictory address before a large crowd that included the governor of Massachusetts.

A newspaper account of the event said that Annie's speech was "spoken in tones that vibrated with true feeling and with genuine refinement." The poor little Irish girl had come a long way from Tewksbury—and she intended to keep it that way. Not until she was in her 60s did she finally tell anyone about her time in the poorhouse.

Still glowing from the applause that followed her speech, Annie returned to her room at Perkins to "shed my white splendor before the supper bell rang." That's when "the thought of money brought me back to reality.... What could I do to get money? Here I was twenty years old, and I realized that I did not know a single subject thoroughly. I could not possibly teach, and I had no urge to teach. I knew better than I had six years ago how abysmal my ignorance was."

Annie spent the summer with Mrs. Hopkins at her home on Cape Cod. She walked along the shore and worried about earning

Shown here at about age 20, Annie graduated from Perkins in 1886. Her favorite class was on Shakespeare. "The impression these plays made upon me was profound.... For the first time I felt the magic of great poetry, the beauty of words, the romance of life."

"We...have the power of controlling the course of our lives. We can educate ourselves; we can, by thought and perseverance, develop all the powers and capacities entrusted to us."

From Annie's valedictory address on June 1, 1886

her living. Then one day a note arrived from Michael Anagnos, the director of Perkins. He had received a letter from a Mr. Arthur Keller in Alabama who was in search of a governess for "his little deaf-mute and blind daughter." Would Annie be interested?

Born on June 27, 1880, in Tuscumbia, Alabama, Helen Keller was able to see and hear as a baby. Then a few months before her second birthday, she suffered a severe illness that left her blind and deaf. Some doctors suggested that it might be best if Helen were put in an institution, but Kate and Arthur Keller refused to shut their daughter away. In time, little Helen learned to use her three remaining senses—touch, smell, and taste—to explore the world around her. She began to express her basic needs by using simple signs. If she wanted bread and butter, for example, she mimicked cutting and buttering a slice of bread.

From feeling their faces when they talked, Helen knew that her family members communicated with each other by moving their lips. Not being able to do the same made her wild with frustration. By age six, she was nearly uncontrollable. She threw tantrums when she didn't get what she wanted. She smashed things on purpose. Once she tipped over her baby sister's cradle while the baby was in it. If Kate had not been there to catch the infant before she hit the floor, she might have died. The Kellers despaired. If they couldn't handle Helen now, how would they ever manage her when she grew older and stronger?

Then one day Helen's mother chanced upon a book called *American Notes,* written some 40 years earlier by English author Charles Dickens. In the book, Dickens wrote about visiting a remarkable deaf-blind girl named Laura Bridgman, who had been taught how to communicate. The story filled Kate with hope. Perhaps Helen, too, could be reached.

The Keller's search for help led them to Dr. Alexander Graham Bell, the inventor of the telephone and a leader in the field of deaf education. Arthur took Helen to Washington, D.C., to meet Bell, who was impressed by the girl's curiosity. Bell suggested that the Kellers contact Michael Anagnos at Perkins to find a teacher for her.

Annie didn't really want to teach, but she desperately needed work. Her worst nightmare was having to go back to Tewksbury. Anything was better than that. And this job paid $25 a month, which seemed like a fortune to her. Annie took the job. To prepare herself for it, she spent the next few months back at Perkins, where she pored over reports of Laura Bridgman's education.

She had never set foot out of Massachusetts before, but Annie Sullivan felt "brave and independent" when she boarded the train for the South. She took with her a gift from the Perkins students to Helen—a doll dressed in an outfit sewn for it by Laura Bridgman. Annie arrived in the small country town of Tuscumbia, Alabama, on March 3, 1887. Helen Keller later described this day as her "soul's birthday."

Kate Keller and her stepson James were waiting at the train station with

"Her house [looks] as though a hurricane had passed over it, around it, and through it. She is careless about everything and yet she is good-hearted and sincere," Annie Sullivan wrote about Kate Keller (above). She described Arthur Keller (top) as "very hospitable," but she found "the arrogance of these southern people...most exasperating.... To hear them talk, you would think that they had won every battle in the Civil War." The letter in the background is from Michael Anagnos to Annie, telling her of the teaching position with the Keller family.

"I became so excited and eager to see my little pupil that I could scarcely sit still in my seat. I felt like getting out and pushing the horse along faster."

The Keller family home, Ivy Green, got its name from the ivy growing all around the property. Next to the main house (background) is the small cottage where Annie and Helen lived by themselves briefly. The inset picture shows the front room of this cottage. Used to institutional life in Boston, Annie was astounded that "the Kellers raised nearly everything we needed — vegetables, fruits, pigs, turkeys, chickens, and lambs."

the carriage. As they drove through Tuscumbia, Annie admired the blossoming fruit trees and the good, earthy smell of plowed fields. She trembled with eagerness to meet her young student.

Helen's father, a retired Confederate army captain and editor of the local newspaper, met them on the lawn of the house, called Ivy Green. Annie had one question for him: "Where is Helen?" Then she saw the girl standing on the porch, with "one hand stretched out, as if she expected someone to come in."

As Annie started up the porch steps, six-year-old Helen rushed toward her with such force that Annie nearly tumbled backward. The girl's busy fingers felt Annie's face and dress and bag, which she tried to open. When Mrs. Keller tried to take the bag away, Helen flew into a rage and began kicking violently. Annie distracted Helen by letting her hold her watch, "and the tempest was over."

One of Helen's many dolls. At Ivy Green, Annie also liked to play with dolls. She didn't have any as a child.

Helen did not stay calm for long, however. In a letter to Mrs. Hopkins, Annie wrote that Helen "is very quick-tempered and willful, and nobody, except her brother James, has attempted to control her…. Dear child, her restless spirit gropes in the dark. Her untaught, unsatisfied hands destroy what-ever they touch because they do not know what else to do with things."

On her very first evening at Ivy Green, Annie started to teach Helen and her "unsatisfied hands." When Helen helped Annie unpack, she found the doll the Perkins girls had sent her. Annie took the oppor-tunity to teach Helen her first word. Using the manual alphabet, she spelled "d-o-l-l" into Helen's hand. The girl quickly learned to mimic the hand signs, but she didn't understand that they meant anything.

A few days later, Annie wrote to Mrs. Hopkins: "I had a battle royal with Helen this morning." The battle scene was the breakfast table. Helen's table manners appalled Annie. The child plunged her hands into others' plates to grab what she wanted, and nobody stopped her. When Annie refused to let Helen take food from her plate, "a contest of wills followed." The rest of the family left the room, and Annie locked the dining-room door. The contest of wills lasted for a couple of hours, but Annie finally succeeded in making Helen eat her own food with her own spoon and fold her napkin, too. "Then I let her out into the warm sunshine and went up to my room and threw myself on the bed exhausted. I had a good cry and felt better."

Another time, when Annie insisted that Helen sit down for a lesson, Helen's "fist flew like lightning and knocked out two of Annie's teeth." A less strong-willed teacher might have fled Ivy Green, but not Annie Sullivan. She never gave up a fight. Also, she knew from the years she had spent at Tewksbury and from her own struggle with blindness what it meant to be an outcast, how it felt to be shut away from the rest of the world. She knew how miserable it was to feel all alone. Her heart went out to this young girl trapped in a world of darkness and silence.

Annie soon realized that "I could do nothing with Helen in the midst of the family, who have always allowed her to do exactly as she pleased.... I saw clearly that it was useless to try to teach her language or anything else until she learned to obey me." So she persuaded the Kellers to let her live alone with Helen for a while.

Annie and Helen moved into a small, vine-covered cottage near the main house. Annie described it as "a genuine bit of paradise," but her first day alone with Helen was anything but heavenly. Just getting her pupil to go to bed took two hours. "I never saw such strength and endurance in a child," Annie wrote. "But fortunately for us both, I am a little stronger, and quite as obstinate when I set out."

Annie needed every bit of her strength and stubbornness over the next few days. One morning Helen refused to get dressed, and Annie refused to let her eat breakfast until she did. When Captain Keller looked in the window around ten o'clock and saw his daughter still in her nightgown and her breakfast uneaten on the table, it distressed him so much that he stormed back to the main house saying he had "a great mind to send that Yankee girl back to Boston." His sister talked him out of it. "Miss Annie is going to be Helen's salvation," Eveline Keller told her brother. "Helen must learn obedience and feel her dependence upon her."

Helen Keller, about age seven. "Helen was made of fingers and curiosity," said Annie. "She kept me on the jump finding answers to her questions."

By the end of their first week in the cottage, Helen had learned just that. "My heart is singing for joy this morning," Annie wrote Mrs. Hopkins on March 20, 1887. "A miracle has happened!… The wild little creature of two weeks ago has been transformed into a gentle child." Somehow, through a combination of patience and firmness, Annie had taught Helen self-control without breaking the young girl's spirit. She had also won her pupil's heart and trust.

Now Helen seemed to enjoy learning new words, although she still didn't know what they meant. One day Captain Keller stopped by the cottage with his dog Belle. Helen sat down beside the dog and began to manipulate its claws. "We couldn't think for a second what she was doing," Annie wrote, "but when we saw her make the letters 'd-o-l-l' on her own fingers, we knew that she was trying to teach Belle to spell."

When the Kellers insisted that Helen and Annie move back to Ivy Green the following week, Annie made a bold demand. "I have told Captain and Mrs. Keller that they must not interfere with me in any way," she wrote Mrs. Hopkins. "Miss Spitfire" did not intend to let Helen's family overindulge her pupil again and undo the progress she had made "at the cost of so much pain and trouble."

Just as Dr. Samuel Gridley Howe had done with Laura Bridgman 50 years earlier, Annie at first kept to a rigid routine of lessons with her student. The same hour every day was devoted to learning new vocabulary words, as she finger-spelled the names of familiar objects into Helen's palm. But Annie didn't stop there. "You mustn't think this is the only time I spell to Helen," she told Mrs. Hopkins, "for I spell in her hand everything we do all day long, although she has no idea as yet what the spelling means." Then in early April, Helen took what Annie called "the second great step in her education. She has learned that everything has a name."

A teacup owned by the Keller family. At first, Helen confused the idea of a cup with the drink inside it.

Annie had taught Helen the spellings for the nouns "mug" and "milk" and for the verb "drink," but Helen kept mixing them up. She didn't understand that they stood for different things. Then, on the morning of April 5, while she was washing up, she pointed to the water and patted Annie's hand. It was Helen's way of asking for the spelling of something. In a letter to Mrs. Hopkins, Annie described what happened next:

"I spelled 'w-a-t-e-r' and thought no more about it until after breakfast. Then it occurred to me that with the help of this new word I might succeed in straightening out the 'mug-milk' difficulty. We went out to the pump-house, and I made Helen hold her mug under the

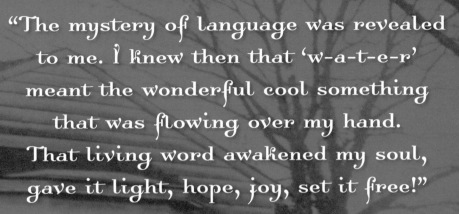

"The mystery of language was revealed to me. I knew then that 'w-a-t-e-r' meant the wonderful cool something that was flowing over my hand. That living word awakened my soul, gave it light, hope, joy, set it free!"

— Helen Keller

The water pump where Annie unlocked the mystery of language for Helen one April morning in 1887 sits between the main house at Ivy Green and the small cottage next to it, shown here. That night, Annie wrote, Helen "kissed me for the first time, and I thought my heart would burst, so full was it of joy."

spout while I pumped. As the cold water gushed forth, filling the mug, I spelled 'w-a-t-e-r' in Helen's free hand. The word coming so close upon the sensation of cold water rushing over her hand seemed to startle her. She dropped the mug and stood as one transfixed. A new light came into her face. She spelled 'water' several times. Then she dropped on the ground and asked for its name."

Helen asked for the names of several more things, then suddenly turned around and asked for Annie's name. Annie spelled "T-e-a-c-h-e-r." It was what Helen would call her for the rest of their lives.

On the way back to the house, Helen asked for the name of everything she touched. By the end of the day, she knew 30 new words. A few days later Annie decided to abandon formal lessons and follow her own instincts for teaching Helen—a brave step for a brand-new teacher. Annie knew that hearing children learned language by imitating what they heard. So she decided that the best way to teach Helen language would be to "talk into her hand as we talk into the baby's ears.... I shall use complete sentences in talking to her, and fill out the meaning with gestures."

From that point on, learning became an exciting adventure, and Annie let Helen's interests lead the way to learning opportunities. No more boring, repetitive classroom lessons for them! Instead, they spent most of their days outdoors. Wherever they roamed, from the barnyard to the banks of the nearby Tennessee River, Annie's lightning-quick fingers danced constantly in Helen's hand, answering her questions and describing the world around them. "I feel as if I had never seen anything until now, Helen finds so much to ask about along the way," Annie wrote. They chased butterflies, and when they caught one Helen would feel it while Annie explained about it in detail. Helen "heard" the squeals of piglets and moos of cows by feeling the vibrations the sounds made in the animals' bodies. Helen later recalled that "everything that could hum, or buzz, or sing, or bloom, had a part in my education."

Annie taught Helen verbs, or action words, by guiding her through the motions of running or jumping or swinging. She taught Helen about laughing by tickling her until she giggled and spelling "l-a-u-g-h" into her palm. Annie was both eyes and ears for Helen, signing into her hand a vivid description of whatever was taking place around them, including what other people were doing or saying.

Helen blossomed under Annie's innovative approach to teaching. By the end of May, she knew more than 300 words and had learned to read words printed in raised type. Then she learned to write with a pencil on paper using a grooved letter board. Helen learned so quickly that Annie, with only six years of schooling, raced to keep up with her pupil. "My mind is undisciplined, full of slips and jumps…. I need a teacher quite as much as Helen," she wrote Mrs. Hopkins after two months in Tuscumbia.

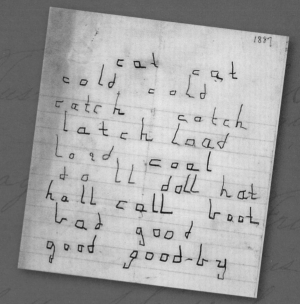

"Our school-room and play-room were identical. The school-room had no hard little seats, no prim little desks, no fixed order — it was out-of-doors. It was not a cage, but the nest from which the bird flies where he likes, and to which it returns at will."

At top is a sample of Helen's writing from June 20, 1887. Annie Sullivan's own handwriting is in the background, in a letter sent to Michael Anagnos on June 19, 1887. In the letter she tells him that Helen "can count up to thirty very quickly and can write seven of the square hand letters and the words which can be made with them."

"In her [Annie's] fingers words rang, rippled, danced, buzzed, and hummed. She made every word vibrant to my mind — she would not let the silence about me be silent."

— Helen Keller

Nonetheless, Annie sensed that she was up to the task. "Something within me tells me that I shall succeed beyond my dreams," she confided.

Eight months after Annie's arrival in Tuscumbia, Captain Keller wrote to Alexander Graham Bell: "It affords me great pleasure to report that [Helen's] progress in learning is phenomenal." Besides learning to spell and read and write, he said, "she has also mastered addition, multiplication and subtraction and is progressing finely with geography."

News about Helen spread fast, thanks in great part to Perkins director Michael Anagnos. He called Helen's achievements a "miracle" and shared Annie's reports to him with the press, which greatly exaggerated the girl's accomplishments. One time Annie fumed that "the truth is not wonderful enough to suit the newspapers; so they enlarge upon it and invent ridiculous embellishments." She was concerned that all the publicity might backfire and harm Helen if the public expected too much of her.

But although Annie claimed, "My beautiful Helen shall not be transformed into a prodigy if I can help it," she was nonetheless excited about her own prospects for fame. "I should think Helen's education would surpass in interest and wonder Dr. Howe's achievement" with Laura Bridgman, she confessed to Mrs. Hopkins. Annie's mixed feelings are understandable. After all, she was barely 21 years old, and she was justly proud of her success as a teacher.

Helen was much more than just a student to Annie, however. After all her lonely years spent living in institutions, Annie rejoiced that she finally had someone to love and care for. She confided to Mrs. Hopkins, "It is a great thing to feel that you are of some use in the world, that you are necessary to somebody. Helen's dependence on me for almost everything makes me strong and glad."

But after a year in Tuscumbia, Annie grew restless. Life in the small town bored her. And although the Kellers were kind, she thought they meddled too much with Helen's education. Annie had grown very possessive of her pupil. Moreover, Annie thought Helen was ready for opportunities beyond what she could provide for her at home in Tuscumbia. So she happily accepted when Michael Anagnos invited them to spend time at Perkins.

In May 1888, Annie and Helen headed for Boston. Never again would they stay with Helen's family for longer than a visit. Although the Kellers—especially Kate—stayed involved in Helen's affairs, for the most part her care would belong to Annie Sullivan for the next 50 years.

On their way north, Annie and Helen stopped in Washington, D.C., for a visit with Alexander Graham Bell. He was delighted to see Helen's progress for himself, and he was eager to ask Annie about her teaching methods. They also visited President Grover Cleveland, the first of several Presidents Annie and Helen would meet in their lifetime.

For the next several years, Annie and Helen spent almost every winter at Perkins, living free of charge as guests of the school. Annie remained Helen's main teacher, but other Perkins teachers also worked with her. Helen asked one teacher to teach her French, and the speed at which she learned the language astounded everybody.

When Helen was ten, she started lessons with a speech teacher. Soon Annie took over the instruction herself. Helen would place her hand on Annie's face to feel the movements and vibrations when she spoke, then try to imitate those sounds herself. "Many times," a cousin of Helen's recalled, "it was necessary for Helen to put her sensitive fingers in Teacher's mouth, sometimes far down her throat, until Teacher would be nauseated, but nothing was too hard, so Helen was benefited."

Helen's fame continued to grow, fueled by Michael Anagnos's glowing reports of the "phenomenal child." People around the world were inspired by her story, by the lovely young girl's victory over darkness and silence. Wealthy Bostonians, eager to meet the wonder girl—and to show her off to their friends—invited her and Annie to parties in their elegant homes. Sweet-faced, open-hearted Helen always enchanted her hosts, many of whom donated big sums to Perkins. With her keen intelligence and quick wit, Annie could be charming, too, but she often felt uncomfortable at such events, and it showed in her scowls. Fiercely proud, she was quick to take offense if she thought she was being treated like a lowly nursemaid instead of an honored teacher. Despite her newfound celebrity as the "miracle worker," Annie still felt insecure and deeply ashamed of her past.

Not everyone thought Annie Sullivan was a miracle worker. Some people believed that Helen Keller didn't really have a mind of her own, that Annie shaped her thoughts. Then something happened when Helen was 11 that seemed to justify these doubts.

Helen, standing at left, poses with other deaf-blind children at Perkins circa 1892. To Helen's delight, almost everyone at Perkins could finger-talk with her. "What joy to talk with other children in my own language!" she later recalled. The background picture shows the Perkins Institution in South Boston.

"It is wonderful how words generate ideas! Every new word Helen learns seems to carry with it the necessity for many more. Her mind grows through its ceaseless activity."

Annie Sullivan speaks aloud to Helen, who can understand what her teacher is saying by feeling the vibrations and movements that Annie's lips and larynx, or voice box, make when she talks. Helen picked up the ability to lip-read with her fingertips during her speech lessons. This photograph was made when Annie was about 29 years old and Helen was about 15.

Annie (far left) and Helen (in plaid coat) at Niagara Falls in March, 1893 (above). With them are two friends. That summer they also traveled to Chicago, where they rode a brand-new invention called the Ferris wheel (right).

Helen was accused of plagiarism—of copying someone else's words or ideas and passing them off as her own. A story she had given Michael Anagnos for his birthday, called "The Frost King," was very similar to one published years earlier. Apparently Helen had heard the story and memorized parts of it without realizing it. The way they were treated over the incident upset Annie and Helen deeply, and it led to the end of their friendship with Anagnos.

In May 1892, Annie and Helen left Perkins for good and returned to Ivy Green. Annie wrote that Helen was "so unlike her own bright self that a great anxiety took possession of my heart." She also worried about money. Captain Keller was so heavily in debt that he could not pay her salary, much less afford to send Helen to another school. Fortunately, Alexander Graham Bell and some of the wealthy friends Annie and Helen had made in Boston stepped in to help support them, so that they could stay together and continue Helen's education.

In 1893, Annie and Helen's friends arranged a trip to Niagara Falls for them. The vibrations from the thundering water astonished Helen. "I had the same feeling once before when I stood by the great ocean and felt its waves beating against the shore," she wrote her mother.

That summer they also visited the World's Columbian Exposition in Chicago, the largest fair that had ever been held. They stayed for three weeks. Alexander Graham Bell himself escorted them around the fair.

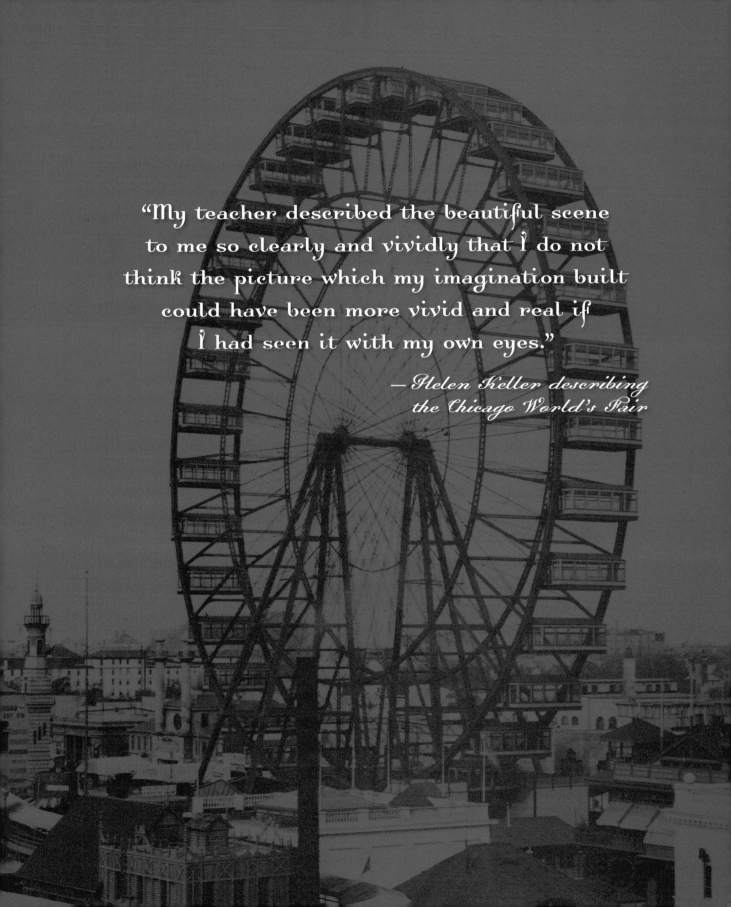

"My teacher described the beautiful scene
to me so clearly and vividly that I do not
think the picture which my imagination built
could have been more vivid and real if
I had seen it with my own eyes."

— Helen Keller describing
the Chicago World's Fair

Thirteen-year-old Helen attracted crowds wherever she went, from the exhibition halls to the breathtaking new contraption called the Ferris wheel. Always by her side was Annie Sullivan, spelling into her hand all the sights and sounds she could not experience for herself. Annie's goal for Helen was for her to live as normal a life as possible. She thought it was important for Helen to meet lots of different people and to have as many unusual experiences as possible. Annie herself also needed frequent changes in their routine. "She was forever seeking an outlet for her restlessness," Helen later wrote. "She believed in going somewhere often and seeing something new."

Bell remained a great friend to both Annie and Helen for the rest of his life. He was one of the few people whose interest did not focus primarily on Helen. He gave Annie the credit she was due. He knew that she was a uniquely gifted teacher, and he believed the techniques she used with Helen could be used to revolutionize educational methods in schools for the deaf. Annie wrote years later that "it was an immense advantage for one of my temper, impatience, and antagonisms to know Dr. Bell intimately over a long period of time. I never felt at ease with anyone until I met him. I was extremely conscious of my crudeness. Dr. Bell had a happy way of making people feel pleased with themselves."

In 1894 Bell asked Annie to speak at a meeting of the American Association to Promote the Teaching of Speech to the Deaf, held in Chautauqua, New York. When the time came, however, she was too shy to deliver the paper she had written. Bell had to read it for her. In it, Annie stated: "We shall never properly develop the higher natures of our little ones while we continue to fill their minds with the so-called rudiments.... Let us lead them during the first years to find their greatest pleasure in nature. Let them run in the fields, learn about animals, and observe real things. Children will educate themselves under right conditions. They require guidance and sympathy far more than instruction." She also claimed, "Children should be encouraged to read for the pure delight of it." Annie's speech was a great success, and it convinced a wider public of her extraordinary talent as a teacher.

Helen and Annie (seated at far left) pose with other students and teachers at the Wright-Humason School for the deaf in New York in 1895.

That fall, Annie and Helen moved to New York City, so that Helen could go to the Wright-Humason School for the deaf and work on her speech and lip-reading. Well-known people in New York clamored to meet Helen. Among them was the popular writer Samuel Clemens, better known as Mark Twain. He became very fond of both Helen and Annie, and he encouraged his wealthy friends to contribute to a fund for Helen's education.

When she was 16, Helen decided that she wanted to go to college, something very few women—let alone a deaf-blind woman—did in those days. She set her heart on Radcliffe College, in Cambridge, Massachusetts. It was the women's branch of Harvard University. Annie knew that Helen would have to attend yet another school to prepare for the Radcliffe entrance exams. And Annie was tired of classrooms and institutions. "Sometimes it seems to me as if I could not endure the thought of going to another school," she wrote a friend. But Annie was also tired of the whispers that she and Helen were frauds. What better way to prove Helen's abilities than for her to earn a college degree?

So Annie and Helen enrolled at a preparatory school for young ladies in Cambridge, Massachusetts. Helen's younger sister, Mildred, joined them. For the first time, Helen attended class with what she called "normal" students—those who could see and hear. Annie went to every class with Helen, signing the lessons into her hand. Few of Helen's textbooks were in braille, so Annie had to read and sign them to Helen, too. "It is harder for Teacher than it is for me," Helen wrote a friend, "because the strain on her poor eyes is so great."

Annie overused her eyes and pushed herself hard for Helen's sake. She pushed Helen hard, too. The school's director, Arthur Gilman, thought that Annie was making Helen sick by insisting that she study so much. He wrote to Helen's mother and convinced her to let him take charge of Helen and separate her from Annie. For a brief time his plan succeeded, until Mrs. Keller arrived in Cambridge and saw how devastated Helen was. She withdrew both her daughters from the school, and Annie and Helen were reunited. Never again would anyone separate them.

The ordeal left Annie badly shaken. It was not the first time she had been accused of overworking Helen. She may have done so. Annie was a brilliant teacher and she was passionately devoted to Helen, but she was far from perfect. She was still hot-tempered and touchy. She was quick to criticize others. She could be impatient and irritable when Helen made mistakes or didn't meet Annie's high standards.

Annie demanded perfection. Not only Helen's reputation but hers, too, was at stake. As she grew older, Helen recognized Annie's faults, her argumentative nature, her dark moods. "In her younger years Teacher was too apt to assume an aggressive attitude in argument," Helen later wrote. "She was inclined to give and take offense. She could be inflexible and proud, and it was a point of honor with her to pound her arguments into those who differed from her instead of trying to win them over with tact." But none of this mattered to Helen. To her, Annie was her beloved Teacher, the one who had opened the world to her and was continuing to give her the world. Gradually, their relationship changed. Annie became less controlling, and Helen more independent-minded. "She [Teacher] ceased to treat me as a child, she did not command me any more," Helen wrote. Helen later went on to support such causes as socialism and women's suffrage, which Annie opposed.

When Helen entered Radcliffe in the fall of 1900, both she and Annie worked harder than ever. Annie interpreted all the professors' lectures and read "a multitude of books" to Helen, from medieval literature to books in advanced

Alarmed by reports that Annie was overworking Helen at school, Kate Keller (top) wrote Annie this letter on November 28, 1897 (background). After telling Annie that she "could not doubt your love for the child," Kate went on to say that "studying all her waking hours" was more than Helen "could safely do." Helen's sister, Mildred, shown above with Helen, also attended the school.

"You are a wonderful creature, the most wonderful in the world — you and your other half together — Miss Sullivan, I mean, for it took the pair of you to make a complete and perfect whole. How she stands out in her letters! Her brilliancy, penetration, originality, wisdom, character...they are all there."

— Mark Twain in letter
to Helen Keller

French and German. All that reading further stressed Annie's eyes, and she consulted a doctor. "When he heard that Teacher read to me five or more hours daily," Helen recalled, the doctor exclaimed, "That is sheer madness, Miss Sullivan. You must rest your eyes completely." But there was no time to rest her eyes. Helen came first, and Annie had to help her keep up with her studies.

One of Helen's college professors, impressed by her writing skills, urged her to write about what she knew best—her own life. This led to the publication of her autobiography, *The Story of My Life*, in 1903. The book became an international best-seller. Mark Twain declared himself charmed by it. Helen dedicated the book to Alexander Graham Bell. Bell was especially excited about one section of it, which featured the weekly letters that Annie had written to Mrs. Hopkins during her first year in Tuscumbia. These letters provided a detailed description of how Annie taught Helen. Dr. Bell wrote to Annie that her let-

Helen Keller converses with Annie Sullivan and Alexander Graham Bell by finger-spelling with Bell and lip-reading with Annie.

ters would "become a standard, the principles that guided you in the early education of Helen are of the greatest importance to all teachers." He went on to say that the letters showed "that Helen's progress was as much due to her teacher as to herself.... It is your duty to use your brilliant abilities as a teacher for the benefit of other teachers."

RADCLIFFE COLLEGE.

MISSION.

is admitted to t

Dean of Radcliffe

Clad in the traditional cap and gown (above) and guided to the stage by Annie Sullivan, Helen Keller received a standing ovation when she graduated from Radcliffe College in 1904. Shown in the background is Helen's certificate of admission to Radcliffe. To prove that Helen's work was really her own, the dean of Radcliffe did not permit Annie to be present when Helen took exams. Someone else had to translate the exam questions into braille for Helen.

In 1904, Helen graduated from Radcliffe College cum laude, which means with honors. She was the first deaf-blind person ever to earn a college degree. Many people, including Helen, thought that Annie Sullivan also deserved a diploma.

Annie and Helen settled into a farmhouse they bought in Wrentham, Massachusetts. They still depended on the generosity of their wealthy friends for support, but they hoped Helen's writing would help them earn their own living.

A frequent visitor to Wrentham was a Harvard teacher and magazine editor named John Macy. He had helped Annie and Helen edit Helen's book. John became good friends with Helen, but he fell madly in love with fiery, fascinating Annie Sullivan. Annie loved him back, but she worried about their age differ-ence—she was 11 years older than John. And of course there was Helen. Annie considered Helen "her very life—her job and her child." But Helen was an adult now. She encouraged Annie to marry John; she wanted her to be happy. John reassured Annie that he under-stood that Helen would always come first.

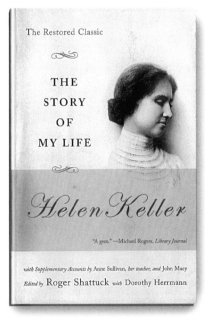

Helen's autobiography, which has been translated into 50 languages. John Macy helped edit the book.

Annie and John married on May 3, 1905, and their first years together were very happy. Both of them helped Helen with her writing, and John published his own poetry and magazine articles. The Wrentham house was often filled with family and friends and lively conversation. But there never seemed to be quite enough money to make ends meet. So in 1913 Annie and Helen went on a lecture tour. They traveled from town to town, appearing in performance halls and theaters across the country.

At their home in Wrentham, Massachusetts, John Macy finger-spells to Helen while Annie gazes over his shoulder at a letter. John had learned the manual alphabet while working with Helen on her autobiography. Not long after her wedding to John in 1905, Annie wrote a friend, "When I realize what has happened to me it seems as if the great happiness which is mine should make me better and wiser in every way." When John left their marriage in 1914, which is around the time this picture was made, it broke Annie's heart.

"One thing is certain, my marriage shall make no difference in my love and care for Helen, and as far as possible I shall share every happiness with her."

"The sweetest, loveliest, happiest home in the world," is how Annie Sullivan described her and Helen's farmhouse in Wrentham, Massachusetts (left). After John Macy married Annie and moved in with the two women, he rigged ropes around the property so that Helen could hold on to them and take a walk outdoors all by herself without getting hurt or lost. One of Annie and Helen's favorite reading spots at Wrentham was amid the branches of a tree (above).

Annie would speak first about how she had taught Helen, and then Helen herself would come on stage and answer questions from the audience. Additional vocal coaching had helped make her speech more understandable. The public was still fascinated by both women, and tickets to their lectures sold well.

Over time, Annie and John's marriage fell apart. Despite his best intentions, John came to resent the way Annie's life centered on Helen.

He spent more and more time away from Wrentham. In 1914 he left for good, and Annie sank into sadness. Not only did she miss John desperately, but her health was poor. She had become very overweight, and her eyesight was worse than ever. Still, she pulled herself together for Helen's sake. There were bills to be paid, so the two of them went on another lecture tour. With them went Polly Thomson, a young Scottish immigrant who had recently joined them as Helen's secretary. Polly learned the manual alphabet so that she could take over some of the reading to Helen, who received stacks of letters every day from friends and admirers.

Annie began to receive more recognition for her contribution to education. In 1915 she was presented with a Teacher's Medal at the Panama-Pacific Exposition in San Francisco. Also honored at the fair was a celebrated Italian educator named Maria Montessori, whose educational philosophy was very similar to Annie's. Dr. Montessori greatly admired Annie. At the event, she commented, "I have been called a pioneer," then pointed to Anne Sullivan Macy and added, "but there is your pioneer."

In 1916, Annie fell ill with what doctors mistakenly thought was tuberculosis, the same disease that had killed her mother and brother. Polly took her to a special hospital in Lake Placid, New York, for treatment, and Helen went to Alabama to stay with her mother. Annie hated the cold, and on impulse she bought tickets to Puerto Rico for herself and Polly. They rented a small shack and stayed for five months—the longest time Annie and Helen were ever apart. The rest did Annie a world of good. She wrote Helen, "One can't help being happy here.... I go to bed every night soaked with sunshine and orange blossoms, and fall to sleep to the...sound of oxen munching banana leaves."

In 1917 the three women moved to Forest Hills, New York, where they lived quietly with their dog Sieglinde, a Great Dane. Then came an exciting invitation: Would they come to Hollywood to make a movie about Helen's life? They did, and they had a grand time in California.

Spotlights illuminate the Panama-Pacific International Exposition in San Francisco, where Annie Sullivan (inset, far right) and Italian educator Maria Montessori (inset, right) were presented with Teacher's Medals in 1915. Annie was honored on a day designated as "Helen Keller Day."

"For years I have known the teacher's one supreme reward, that of seeing the child she has taught grow into a living force in the world. And today has brought me the happiness of knowing that my work is an inspiration to other teachers."

— from Annie's speech at the 1915 Panama-Pacific Exposition

While legendary actor Charlie Chaplin points to something in front of them, Annie finger-spells into Helen's hand. Seated at Helen's right is Polly Thomson, who became Helen's secretary in 1914. The three women met Chaplin in 1918, when they went to Hollywood, California, to make a movie about Helen's life. A poster for the movie (bottom), billed Helen as the "8th Wonder of the World."

Annie, Helen, and Polly met several movie stars. Actor Charlie Chaplin took a special shine to Annie.

The film, called *Deliverance,* opened in theaters in August 1919. Annie and Helen hoped it would earn them enough money to ease their financial problems. They had some income from Helen's writing and from funds set up for them by wealthy friends, but both women were careless with money. They spent a lot on expensive clothes, vacations, and gifts for friends and the needy. Annie once admitted, "I never think about money until I haven't any."

The movie, however, made almost no money. So to pay their bills, Annie and Helen turned to a new career: They became performers in a kind of traveling variety show known as vaudeville. Some people were horrified that the famous Helen Keller appeared on the same stage as acrobats, tap dancers, and trained seals. Annie herself felt embarrassed, but Helen was proud that they were earning their own living. Audiences loved

"What a marvelous thing is language! How seldom we give it a thought! Yet it is one of the most amazing facts in life. By means of the spoken or written word, thought leaps over the barrier that separates mind from mind."

Helen Keller and Annie Sullivan, pictured here on stage in 1919, entertained audiences in vaudeville theaters across the United States for about three years, from 1919 until 1922. (The theater in the background image was located in New York City.) Especially popular was the question-and-answer period following the two women's act. Helen's witty replies delighted the crowds. When an audience member asked her if she ever thought of marrying, for example, Helen answered, "Yes, are you proposing to me?"

In the photo at left, taken around 1930, Annie Sullivan speaks the words into a recording machine as Helen Keller finger-spells a letter or speech into her hand. A typist would later type out the document. Annie and Helen's work on behalf of the blind and deaf-blind required them to write many letters. In the picture below, taken in 1919 at a hospital for blinded soldiers, Helen offers comfort and encouragement to a soldier who lost his sight during World War I. Polly Thomson, Annie, and a Red Cross official walk behind her.

them, and the vaudeville producers paid them very well, sometimes as much as $2,000 a week.

Their "dignified act," as Helen called it, was basically the same as it had been on the lecture tour. Helen enjoyed the shows and the excitement very much, but Annie found it all exhausting. Her health was poor, and the glare of the stage lights hurt her eyes, which were weaker than ever. They stopped touring in 1922 and returned to Forest Hills.

In 1924 Annie and Helen finally gained financial security when the American

Foundation for the Blind (AFB) hired them to be ambassadors for the organization. Throughout their life together, Annie and Helen had always made time to support causes that helped improve the quality of life for other people with disabilities. Now they would be paid for helping others. Their task for the AFB was to raise public awareness about the needs of the blind and to raise funds to support its programs. They both took to the job with a passion.

When Helen decided to write the second volume of her autobiography, her publisher sent a young editor named Nella Braddy to help her and Annie with it. Nella spent countless hours talking to Annie. It was to her that Annie first confided the haunting details of her childhood, including her years in the poorhouse in Tewksbury. With Annie's permission, Nella wrote her biography. It is the main source of information about Annie's early years.

By 1929, Annie's right eye hurt her so much that doctors removed it. Now she could barely see at all. Nonetheless, in the spring of 1930 she, Helen, and Polly set sail on the first of several trips they made to Europe over the next few years. In 1932 Annie accepted an honorary degree from Temple University in Philadelphia for her contributions to education. Although Annie was the one being honored, as usual

An excellent horseback rider, Annie Sullivan was also a gifted writer, as her letters and speeches reveal. She loved art, music, poetry, and animals, especially dogs. In this picture, taken when she was about 50, she holds one of the many dogs she and Helen had during their lives together. Friends said Annie taught her Great Dane, Sieglinde, to say "Ma-ma" and "wah-ter."

This photograph from 1912 captures Annie Sullivan in a reflective mood. When she died in 1936, newspapers around the world carried the story. The New York Times quoted from the eulogy delivered at her funeral service: "Through [Annie Sullivan's] remarkable work, her friend became a world figure, bringing new confidence in the capacity of the human being to overcome his obstacles. Yet all the while the teacher remained in the background, quiet and truly great.... The consequences of her work will be a shining beacon to blind people all over the world for generation after generation."

the reporters flocked about Helen. "Even at my coronation Helen is queen," Annie noted.

Over the next four years, Annie grew frailer, and she gradually lost what little sight she had left. Now Helen tried to teach Teacher to read braille—the system had changed since Annie learned it—but Annie rebelled. "Helen is and always has been thoroughly well behaved in her blindness as well as her deafness, but I'm making a futile fight of it, like a bucking bronco," Annie told a friend. "It's not the big things in life that one misses through loss of sight, but such little things as being able to read. And I have no patience, like Helen, for the braille system, because I can't read fast enough."

When Anne Sullivan Macy died on October 20, 1936, at the age of 70, 56-year-old Helen Keller was holding her hand, the hand that had spelled the world to Helen for nearly half a century. Annie's ashes were laid to rest in the National Cathedral in Washington, D.C. She was the first teacher and the first woman to be so honored.

Annie and Helen's lives had been so intertwined for so long that it was hard to know where one woman left off and the other picked up. Many people worried that Helen could not carry on without her Teacher. But as Annie had always known, Helen had a mind of her own. Annie had devoted all her adult life to making her beloved pupil strong and free, and Helen went on to live a courageous life dedicated to serving others. Always, Helen gave Annie credit for all she accomplished. "People think Teacher has left me," Helen said years after Annie's death, "but she is with me all the time."

Anne Bancroft and Patty Duke re-create Annie Sullivan and Helen Keller's breakfast-table battle in this scene from the 1962 movie *The Miracle Worker*. The film was adapted from a drama by William Gibson, who based his script on the letters Annie Sullivan wrote to Mrs. Hopkins from Tuscumbia during her first months there.

Afterword

Annie Sullivan's groundbreaking work with Helen Keller continues to inspire teachers today. Indeed, she is considered one of the greatest teachers of all time. Her child-centered philosophy of education, with its emphasis on nature and everyday experiences, is central to many schools today. And many of the methods she developed with Helen more than a century ago are still used by teachers of the deaf-blind, especially her practice of "talking" into Helen's hand the way an adult talks to a hearing baby. (Today there are estimated to be between 40,000 and 70,000 deaf-blind people in the U.S., with varying degrees of hearing and vision loss.)

Annie not only freed Helen from a world of silence and darkness, together they showed the world what a person with severe physical disabilities can accomplish. Helen's academic achievements, her determination to be as self-sufficient as possible, and her zest for life made her a role model for physically challenged people everywhere. Together, Annie and Helen worked to expand educational opportunities and improve the quality of life for all individuals with disabilities, and they raised thousands of dollars to help the blind and deaf-blind.

One sure sign of Annie's success as a teacher was that Helen continued to live a full and meaningful life without her. After Annie's death in 1936, Helen traveled the world as she continued to work on behalf of the blind and deaf-blind. With her went Polly Thomson, whom Annie had trained to assume her role as Helen's companion.

Over the years, Helen's fame grew greater than ever, but Annie Sullivan was not totally forgotten. The story of how the devoted young

Dedicating the Anne Sullivan Macy Memorial Fountain at Radcliffe College in 1960, Helen Keller spoke one word. It was "water," the word that helped Annie teach her that "everything has a name, and that the manual alphabet is the key to everything she wants to know."

teacher taught a half-wild child to communicate kept its grip on the public imagination. Playwright William Gibson brought this story to life in his drama *The Miracle Worker.* Later made into a movie, the play opened on Broadway in 1959 and was a smash hit. It is still performed around the world.

The Miracle Worker focused on Annie Sullivan, not Helen Keller. But Anne Bancroft, the actress who first played Annie on Broadway, found to her dismay that theatergoers gave their most enthusiastic applause to Patty Duke, the young actress who played Helen. Annie Sullivan would not have been surprised by that. She was used to Helen being the crowd-pleaser. (Even the title of this book features Helen's name first, to get people's attention.)

Helen Keller died in 1968 at the age of 87. Her ashes were placed in the National Cathedral next to those of her beloved Teacher. In 1973 Helen was inducted into the National Women's Hall of Fame. Not until 2003 did Annie Sullivan receive the same honor, long overdue.

Toward the end of her life, Annie Sullivan remarked, "I have never known...the deep joy of surrender to my own...individual bent or powers. I have been compelled to pour myself into the spirit of another and to find satisfaction in the music of an instrument not my own and to contribute to the mastery of that instrument by another." Annie gave most of her life to Helen Keller, but she did not regret it. "We do not, I think, choose our destiny," she said. "It chooses us."

Chronology

April 14, 1866
Annie Sullivan is born in Feeding Hills, Massachusetts.

1874
Annie's mother, Alice Sullivan, dies.

February 1876
Annie and her brother, Jimmie, are sent to the Tewksbury Almshouse. Jimmie dies a few months later.

1880
Annie is admitted to the Perkins Institution for the Blind in Boston.

June 27, 1880
Helen Keller is born in Tuscumbia, Alabama.

June 1, 1886
Annie graduates from Perkins as valedictorian of her class.

March 3, 1887
Annie Sullivan arrives in Tuscumbia, Alabama, to teach Helen Keller.

April 5, 1887
Annie has a breakthrough teaching moment with Helen at the water pump when Helen first connects the word "w-a-t-e-r" to the "cool something" flowing over her hand.

1888
Annie and Helen arrive at Perkins Institution for the Blind in Boston as guests of director Michael Anagnos. They spend much of their time here over the next four years.

1894
Annie and Helen move to New York so Helen can attend Wright-Humason School for the deaf to study speech.

1900
With Annie at her side, Helen enters Radcliffe College.

1904
Annie and Helen move to Wrentham, Massachusetts, after Helen graduates from Radcliffe.

May 3, 1905
Annie Sullivan marries John Macy.

1914
Annie and John Macy separate after their marriage fails.

Polly Thomson joins Annie and Helen as Helen's secretary.

1916
Annie and Polly go to Puerto Rico and stay for five months. It is the longest time Annie and Helen are ever apart.

1917
Annie, Helen, and Polly move to Forest Hills, New York.

1918
Annie, Helen, and Polly go to Hollywood to make a movie about Helen's life.

1920
Annie and Helen begin touring with a vaudeville show.

1924
Annie and Helen begin work for the American Foundation for the Blind.

1932
Annie receives an honorary degree from Temple University.

October 20, 1936
Anne Sullivan Macy dies.

June 1, 1968
Helen Keller dies.

Page from a comic book featuring the story of Annie and Helen, circa 1945

Resources

BOOKS

Braddy, Nella (Henney). *Anne Sullivan Macy: The Story behind Helen Keller.* Garden City, New York: Doubleday, Doran & Company, 1933.

Gray, Charlotte. *Reluctant Genius: Alexander Graham Bell and the Passion for Invention.* New York: Arcade Publishing, 2006.

Hermann, Dorothy. *Helen Keller: A Life.* New York: Alfred A. Knopf, 1998.

Hickok, Lorena A. *The Touch of Magic: The Story of Helen Keller's Great Teacher, Anne Sullivan Macy.* New York: Dodd, Mead & Co., 1961.

Keller, Helen. *The Story of My Life.* (edited by Roger Shattuck with Dorothy Hermann). New York: W. W. Norton & Company, 2003.

Keller, Helen. *Teacher: Anne Sullivan Macy.* New York: Dolphin Books, 1955.

Lash, Joseph P. *Helen and Teacher: The Story of Helen Keller and Anne Sullivan Macy.* New York: Delacorte Press, 1980.

U.S. postage stamp issued in 1980.

BOOKS

WRITTEN ESPECIALLY FOR YOUNG READERS

Dash, Joan. *The World at Her Fingertips: The Story of Helen Keller.* New York: Scholastic Press, 2001.

Davidson, Margaret. *Helen Keller's Teacher.* New York: Scholastic Paperbacks, reissue edition, 1992.

Lawlor, Laurie. *Helen Keller: Rebellious Spirit.* New York: Holiday House, 2001.

Selden, Bernice. *The Story of Annie Sullivan: Helen Keller's Teacher.* Milwaukee: Gareth Stevens, 1997.

WEB SITES

Alexander Graham Bell Family Papers
Library of Congress, Manuscript Division
http://memory.loc.gov/ammem/bellhtml/bellhome.html
Contains correspondence between Bell and Annie Sullivan and Helen Keller

Anne Sullivan Macy: Miracle Worker
American Foundation for the Blind
www.afb.org/annesullivan/
Full of fascinating information and pictures. Includes a link to a film clip of Annie and Helen demonstrating how Helen learned to speak

The Helen Keller Foundation for Research and Education
www.helenkellerfoundation.org
A foundation that works to end blindness and deafness through medical research

Helen Keller Kids Museum Online
American Foundation for the Blind
www.afb.org/braillebug/hkmuseum.asp
A fun and informative site

Perkins History Museum
Perkins School for the Blind
www.perkins.org/museum
The profile of Annie Sullivan by B. L. McGinnity, J. Seymour-Ford, and K. J. Andries was especially helpful.

FILM

"The Miracle Worker." MGM. 1962. This wonderful movie is one of my favorites, although it stretches the truth in places. In the movie, Helen utters "wa-wa" when she makes the connection between the water flowing over one hand and the letters Annie is signing into her other palm. In reality, she did not speak.

OTHER MATERIALS

Nella Braddy Henney Collection
Samuel P. Hayes Research Library at the Perkins School for the Blind, Watertown, Massachusetts

Includes notes and journals from Nella Braddy, Annie Sullivan's first biographer, as well as scribbled fragments of notes by Annie

PLACES TO VISIT

Ivy Green
300 West North Commons
Tuscumbia, Alabama 35674
(256) 383-4066
www.helenkellerbirthplace.org
The birthplace of Helen Keller. You can actually touch the water pump where Annie had her breakthrough experience with Helen.

Perkins School for the Blind History Museum
175 North Beacon Street
Watertown, Massachusetts 02472
617-972-7767
www.perkins.org/museum
In addition to exhibits about Annie Sullivan and Helen Keller, this small museum features a variety of fascinating exhibits on the education of the blind and deaf-blind. Perkins moved from Boston to Watertown in 1912. Its name changed from Perkins Institution to Perkins School in 1955.

Credits and Source Notes

Quotations from Annie Sullivan and others are taken from the following sources, which are fully cited on page 62:

Page 5: *The Story of My Life,* by Helen Keller (HKSML), Page 6: *Teacher*, by Helen Keller, p.129; p. 156; Page 9: Nella Braddy Henney Collection, Perkins School for the Blind (PSB); Page 10: "so pretty..." PSB; Page 12: "Jimmy used to tease..." *Anne Sullivan Macy*, by Nella Braddy, p. 22; "I must have been asleep..." Braddy, pp. 26-28; "Very much of what I remember..."www.afb.org/annesullivan/ (AFB); "bright colors..." *Helen Keller: A Life* by Dorothy Hermann, p. 32; Page 13: "My head aches..." PSB; "Mr. Sanborn..." AFB; "like a round peg..." PSB; Page 14: "brain awake..." PSB; "Because I was ignorant..." PSB; Page 16: "When I made mistakes..." PSB; Page 17: PSB; Page 18: "spoken in tones..." *Helen and Teacher*, by Joseph Lash, p. 37; "shed my white..." PSB; "thought of money..." Lash, 38-39; "impression these plays..." AFB; Page 19: PSB; Page 20: "little deaf-mute..." AFB; Page 21: "brave and independent" Hermann, p. 39; "her house...a hurricane..." PSB; "the arrogance..." AFB; Page 22: "I became so excited..." AFB; "the Kellers raised..." Braddy, p. 129; Page 23: "one hand stretched..." AFB; "tempest" AFB; "very quick-tempered..." HKSML, p. 138; Page 24: "battle royal..." HKSML, pp. 141-142; "fist flew..." *Teacher*, by Helen Keller, p. 24; "I could do nothing..." HKSML, p. 142; "bit of paradise" and "I never saw..." HKSML, pp. 143-144; Page 25: "a great mind..." Lash, p. 53; "My heart..." HKSML, pp. 145-146; "We couldn't think..." HKSML, p. 147; "Helen was made..." PSB; Page 26: "I have told Captain..." HKSML, p. 147; "You mustn't think..." HKSML, p. 149; "I spelled w-a-t-e-r..." HKSML, p. 150; Page 27: "mystery of language..." HKSML, p. 27; "kissed me..." HKSML, p. 150; Page 28: "Our school room..." PSB; "can count up to thirty..." Lash, p. 61; Page 29: "talk into her hand..." HKSML, p. 151; "I feel as if..." HKSML, p. 155; "everything that could hum..." HKSML, pp. 35-36; "my mind is undisciplined..." HKSML, p. 159; Page 30: Teacher, p. 47; Page 31: "language of her country..." Hermann, p. 95; "head and fingers ached" HKSML, p. 177; "It affords me..." Reluctant Genius, by Charlotte Gray, p. 270; "truth is not wonderful..." HKSML, p. 132; "My beautiful Helen..." HKSML, p. 159; "a great thing to feel..." HKSML, p. 176; Page 32: "it was necessary for Helen..." Lash, p. 77; Page 33: "phenomenal child" Lash, p. 131; "What joy to talk..." HKSML, p. 42; Page 34: HKSML, p. 155; Page 36: "so unlike her own..." Hermann, p. 89; "stood by the great ocean..." HKSML, p. 338; Page 37:http://memory.loc.gov/ammem/bellhtml/bellhome.html; Page 38: "She was forever seeking..." Teacher, p. 65; "immense advantage..." AFB; "never properly develop..." HKSML, p. 212; Page 39: "Sometimes it seems to me..." Lash, p. 200; Page 40: "harder for Teacher..." HKSML, p. 353; "In her younger years..." Teacher, p. 56; Page 41: "ceased to treat me..." Teacher, p. 56; Page 42: AFB; Page 43: "sheer madness..." Teacher, p. 63; "become a standard..." AFB; Page 45: "her very life..." Hermann, p. 141; Page 46: Lash, p. 331; Page 47: Lash, p. 335; Page 48: "sweetest, loveliest..." Lash, p. 335; Page 49: "pioneer..." Lash, p. 418; "sunshine and orange blossoms..." AFB; Page 50: Lash, p. 421; Page 51: Lash, p. 419; Page 52: "never think about money..." Hermann, p. 235; Page 53: "By means of the spoken word..." Braddy, p. 166; "are you proposing..." Lash, p. 490; Page 56: PSB; Page 57: "at my coronation..." Hermann, p. 251; "bucking bronco..." Hermann, p. 232; "People think teacher..." Teacher, p. 16; Page 60: "everything has a name..." HKSML, p. 149; "I have never known..." AFB.

Credits Key

AFB: Courtesy of the American Foundation for the Blind, Helen Keller Archives

HKBF: Janice Mask Williams, Colbert County Tourism & Convention Bureau, Tuscumbia, Alabama/ Helen Keller Birthplace Foundation

PSB: Courtesy of Perkins School for the Blind

RIH: Whitman Studio, courtesy Radcliffe Archives, Radcliffe Institute, Harvard University

Front cover: AFB; Front cover background; AFB; Spine: AFB; Back cover: AFB; 1: Braille transcription by Cat's Meow Braille Transcription, Wichita, KS; 2-3: AFB; 5: PSB; 6: © Corbis; 9: AFB; 9 (background): Eon Images; 10: Eon Images; 11 (all): Images courtesy of the Public Health Museum, Tewksbury, Massachusetts; 14 (top): Emmet Collection, Miriam and Ira D. Wallach Division of Art, Prints and Photographs,New York Public Library, Astor, Lenox and Tilden Foundations; 14 (bottom): The Granger Collection, New York; 14 (background): AFB; 15: © Jacques Boyer / Roger-Viollet / The Image Works ; 16-17: PSB; 19: AFB; 21 (top and bottom) : Walter Sanders/Time Life Pictures/Getty Images; 21 (background): AFB; 22: Alan Briere / Superstock; 22 (background): Walter Sanders/Time Life Pictures/Getty Images; 23: HKBF; 25: PSB; 26: HKBF; 27: AFB; 29 (all): AFB; 30: AFB; 33: PSB; 33 (background): The Museum of disABILITY History, Williamsville, N.Y.; 34-35: CSU Archives/Everett Collection; 36: AFB; 37: The Granger Collection, New York; 39: AFB; 41 (top): AFB; 41 (bottom): PSB; 41 (background): AFB; 42: Courtesy of the American Foundation for the Blind, Helen Keller Archives; 43: AFB; 44 (all): AFB; 45: From THE STORY OF MY LIFE by Helen Keller, edited by Roger Shattuck. Copyright © 2003 by Roger Shattuck. Used by permission of W.W. Norton & Company, Inc.; 46-47: RIH; 48 (all): AFB; 50-51: © Schenectady Museum; Hall of Electrical History Foundation/Corbis; 51 (left): Hulton Archive/Getty Images; 51 (right): RIH; 52 (top): PSB; 52 (bottom): © Bettmann/Corbis; 53: © Bettmann/Corbis; 53 (background): © Underwood & Underwood/Corbis; 54 (top): PSB; 54 (bottom): AFB; 55: AFB; 56: RIH; 58: ZUMA/United Artists/Newscom; 60: Courtesy Radcliffe Archives, Radcliffe Institute, Harvard University; 61: AFB; 62: AP Photo/USPS.

Index

Educational Extensions

1. How did Annie Sullivan act as "Helen's eyes"? Support your answer by summarizing events from March 3, 1887, to October 20, 1936, and citing evidence from the text.

2. What is resilience? How did Helen Keller and Annie Sullivan display resilience? What does resiliency teach you about your own life? Use both personal examples and examples from the text to support your answers.

3. Annie Sullivan has often been called "the miracle worker." Using evidence from the story, explain how Annie's life prepared her for this quest. Why was she driven to break through Helen's dark and silent world?

4. Annie Sullivan said, "We … have the power of controlling the course of our lives. We can educate ourselves, we can, by thought and perseverance, develop all the powers and capacities entrusted to us." What did she mean by this and what can you learn from this message?

More to ponder …

· What does it mean to be successful?

· Describe the success of a person who you read about.

· How does reading about others' accomplishments inspire you?

· Research a topic from the book. Compare and contrast information and details that you found from different sources.

· How do people change the world?

· How can you make a lasting impact on society?